LEARN TO DRAW
THE BEST OF
nickelodeon ™

With illustrations by Steve Crespo, Shane L. Johnson, Heather Martinez, Warner McGee, Niño Navarra, and Gregg Schigiel

Walter Foster Jr.

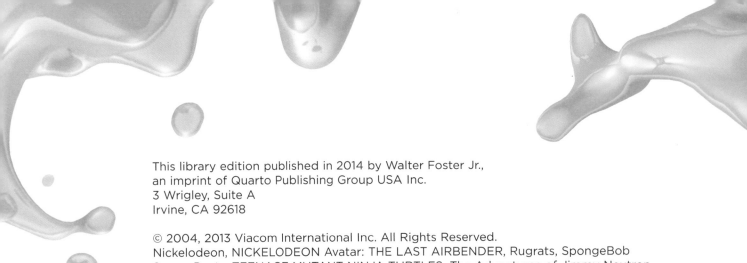

This library edition published in 2014 by Walter Foster Jr.,
an imprint of Quarto Publishing Group USA Inc.
3 Wrigley, Suite A
Irvine, CA 92618

Distributed in the United States and Canada by
Lerner Publisher Services
241 First Avenue North
Minneapolis, MN 55401 U.S.A.
www.lernerbooks.com

First Library Edition

Library of Congress Cataloging-in-Publication Data

Learn to draw the best of Nickelodeon / with illustrations by Steve Crespo, Shane
L. Johnson, Heather Martinez, Warner McGee, Niño Navarra, and Gregg Schigiel. --
Library edition.
     pages cm
ISBN 978-1-93958-119-8
1. Cartoon characters--Juvenile literature. 2. Drawing--Technique--Juvenile literature.
I. Crespo, Steve, illustrator. II. Johnson, Shane L., illustrator. III. Martinez, Heather, illus-
trator. IV. McGee, Warner, illustrator. V. Navarra, Nino, illustrator. VI. Schigiel, Gregg,
illustrator. VII. Nickelodeon (Television network)
  NC1764.L3525 2014
  741.5'1--dc23

                                                                    2013025003

052014
18779

9 8 7 6 5 4 3 2

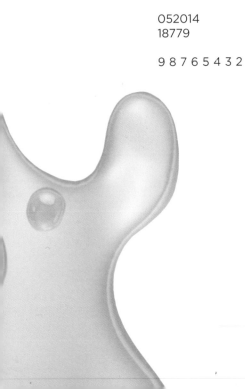

TABLE OF CONTENTS

TOOLS & MATERIALS

Before you begin drawing, you will need to gather the right tools.
Start with a regular pencil, an eraser, and a pencil sharpener.
When you're finished sketching, you can bring your favorite
Nickelodeon characters to life by adding color with felt-tip markers,
colored pencils, crayons, or even paint!

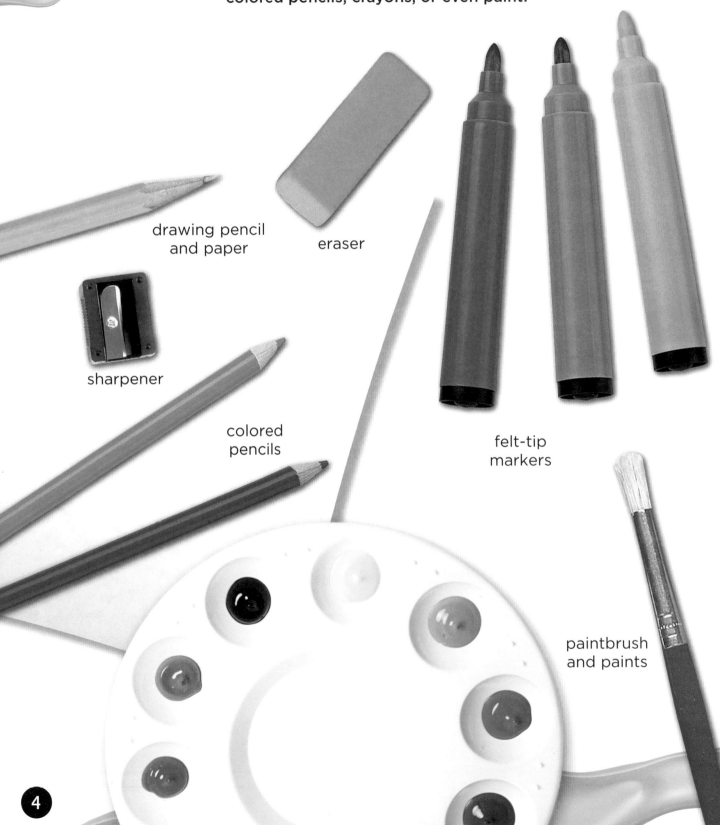

drawing pencil
and paper

eraser

sharpener

colored
pencils

felt-tip
markers

paintbrush
and paints

HOW TO USE THIS BOOK

You don't need a Fairy Godparent to follow these simple steps!

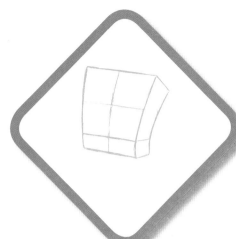

STEP 1

First draw the basic shapes using light lines that will be easy to erase.

STEP 2

Each new step is shown in blue, so you'll know what to add next.

STEP 3

Follow the blue lines to draw the details.

STEP 4

Now darken the lines you want to keep, and erase the rest.

STEP 5

Use fairy magic (or crayons or markers) to add color to your drawing!

5

SPONGEBOB SQUAREPANTS

See the "dots" pattern?

1

2

SpongeBob lives in a fully furnished pineapple under the sea with his pet snail Gary. When he's not working hard at The Krusty Krab, he has a lot of interests that keep him occupied: jellyfishing, bubble art, and karate. His never-ending good nature and enthusiasm can often irritate others, but his refreshing attitude makes him a likable underdog. Despite all of his positive traits, "SpongeBob excitement" usually means "SpongeBob disaster." In the end, though, SpongeBob always wins—even if only for himself.

3

7

6 bumps

1
2
3
4
5
6

1
2
3

3 bumps

Nope!

Keep those teeth
straight!

Yep!

9

SpongeBob is the most dedicated employee at The Krusty Krab—he likes his uniform so much that he never takes it off (not even in the shower!). His biggest dream is to capture the prized "Employee of the Month" award—he has won every month.

3 freckles per cheek

Socks with
2 stripes

4

5

PATRICK STAR

Patrick is SpongeBob's dim-witted yet loyal best friend. His hobbies include sleeping and lying still. This starfish truly idolizes SpongeBob, and together they make a mess of things for everyone around them—but always without meaning to. Part sloth and part dude, Patrick's biggest ambition in life is "uh . . . I . . . uh . . . forget."

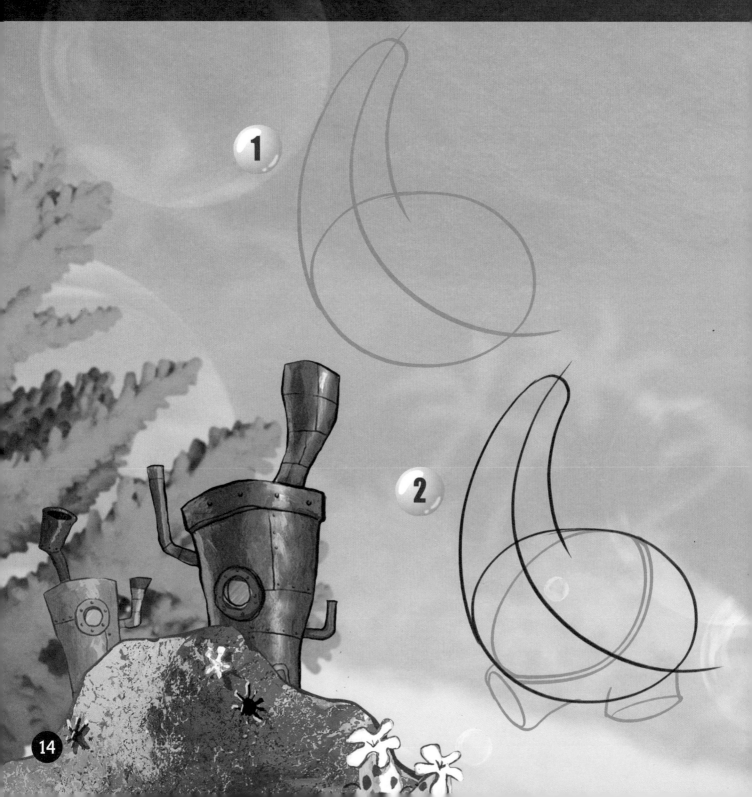

Patrick's body is pear-shaped

Eyebrows are like a squashed letter "z"

3

PLANKTON

Plankton owns Plankton's Chum Bucket, The Krusty Krab's rival. And business isn't good. Boastful and mean, Plankton is constantly plotting ways to steal the famous Krabby Patty recipe.

4 cross pieces

1
2
3
4

"I'm about 2 heads tall" (but don't forget my feet!)

1
2

6

7

MR. KRABS

Mr. Krabs is the greedy owner of The Krusty Krab and SpongeBob's money-hungry boss. Though he finds SpongeBob a constant source of aggravation, Mr. Krabs genuinely likes him. The only thing more valuable to Mr. Krabs than cold, hard cash is his teenage daughter Pearl.

4

Hole

Nose has 2 peaks and 2 valleys

1 2
  2
1

5

6

GARY

SpongeBob often confides in his favorite companion and pet—Gary, the snail. Gary may meow like a cat, but the slimy trail he leaves behind definitely proves he's a mollusk.

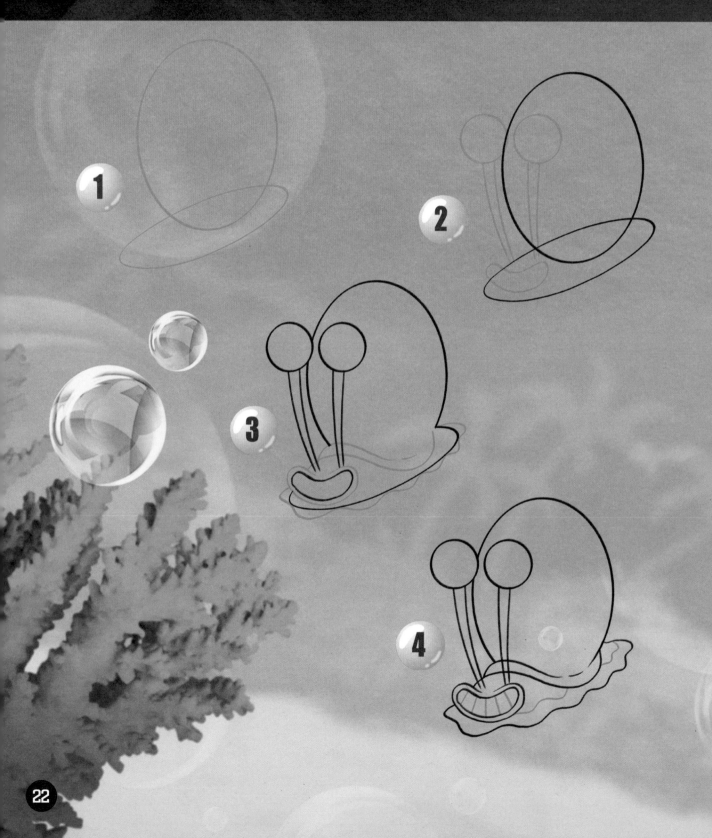

TOMMY PICKLES

Tommy is a born leader. He's smart, loves adventure, and has a special way of charming others (grownups and babies alike). Tommy runs the show—and convinces the others that "a baby's gotta do what a baby's gotta do."

Tommy's fingers look a lot like mini sausages

Tommy has
7 tiny hairs

CHUCKIE FINSTER

Part worrywart and part fraidy cat, Chuckie is one nervous little guy. This stuffy-nosed tot is the Rugrats' voice of caution. The Rugrats can always count on Chuckie to warn everyone about the dangers of, well, everything!

Chuckie's hair looks like candle flames

Chuckie's freckles form a triangle shape

TIMMY

Timmy Turner is pretty smart, is highly imaginative, and has a short attention span. Basically he's your average 10-year-old boy ... sort of. What's different about Timmy? When he says, "I wish," his Fairy Godparents grant it—even if they don't always hear him correctly!

YES! Facial features all stay within shape of head

NO! Eyes and mouth should not extend beyond face

STEP 2

STEP 3

YES! Timmy's hat follows the curve of his head

YES! Hat button floats

STEP 4

STEP 5

Timmy's (and Cosmo's) eyebrows don't curve

YES! Straight, rectangular shapes

NO! Not curved lines

COSMO

It's a good thing Timmy has not one, but two Fairy Godparents! Cosmo means well, but to be frank, most of the time he has no idea what he's doing in the magic department. But what he lacks in ability, he makes up for with his great sense of humor, boundless energy, and endless good mood.

STEP 1

When Cosmo (or Wanda) is floating at rest, the body has a simple shape and front leg fits within shape

STEP 2

Godparents have pupils and noses that are more pointed than Timmy's

Godparents

Timmy

STEP 3

YES! Crown floats above head and lines up with side of head

NO! Crown doesn't touch head or shift left

STEP 4

STEP 5

YES! Cosmo's tie has a straight end and always lies flat

NO! Tie does not move

NO! End is not pointed

WANDA

Sure, Wanda is a bit on the zany side, but she's the most practical and capable half of Timmy's Godparent duo. Wanda loves using her "powers" to make things better, even if that means fixing one of Cosmo's slip-ups. But her major focus is on making sure that Timmy is happy and well taken care of.

When Wanda or Cosmo are fish, they look identical except for face details

PLACE FACE HERE

STEP 3

STEP 4

There are many different ways to show magical powers in action (you can even make up your own!)

WISH!

STEP 5

Wanda's eyelashes extend past her head

When her mouth is closed, top and bottom lips don't line up

JIMMY NEUTRON

What's it like being a 10-year-old super genius? Just ask Jimmy Neutron—Retroville's one-of-a-kind whiz kid. His incredible inventions, formulas, and gadgets help save the world (after almost destroying it) more times than he can count!

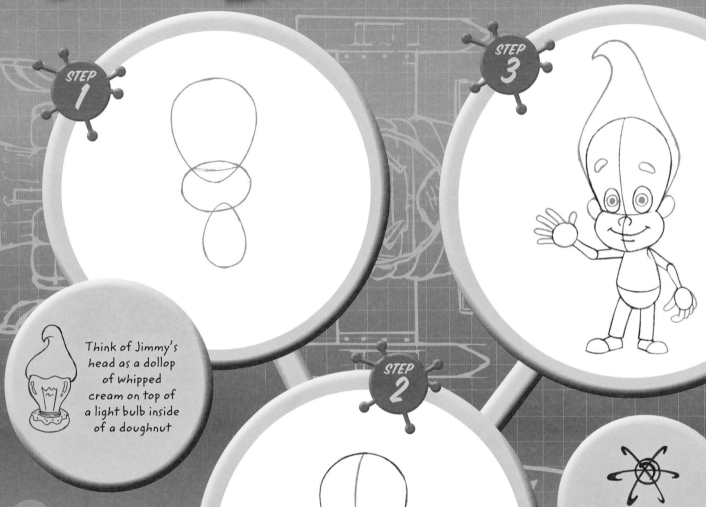

STEP 1

Think of Jimmy's head as a dollop of whipped cream on top of a light bulb inside of a doughnut

STEP 2

STEP 3

Jimmy's chest symbol looks like Saturn, with 3 rings

STEP 4

STEP 5

Jimmy's hair changes shape in reaction to extreme movements

LEONARDO

Leo is a stand-up guy and master of the katana, the most legendary and noble of Japanese weapons. A born leader, Leonardo is learning from Splinter how to guide and inspire his brothers. And it works. Usually. Well, sometimes.

1

2

Legs and arms are tubes that flare out at the base

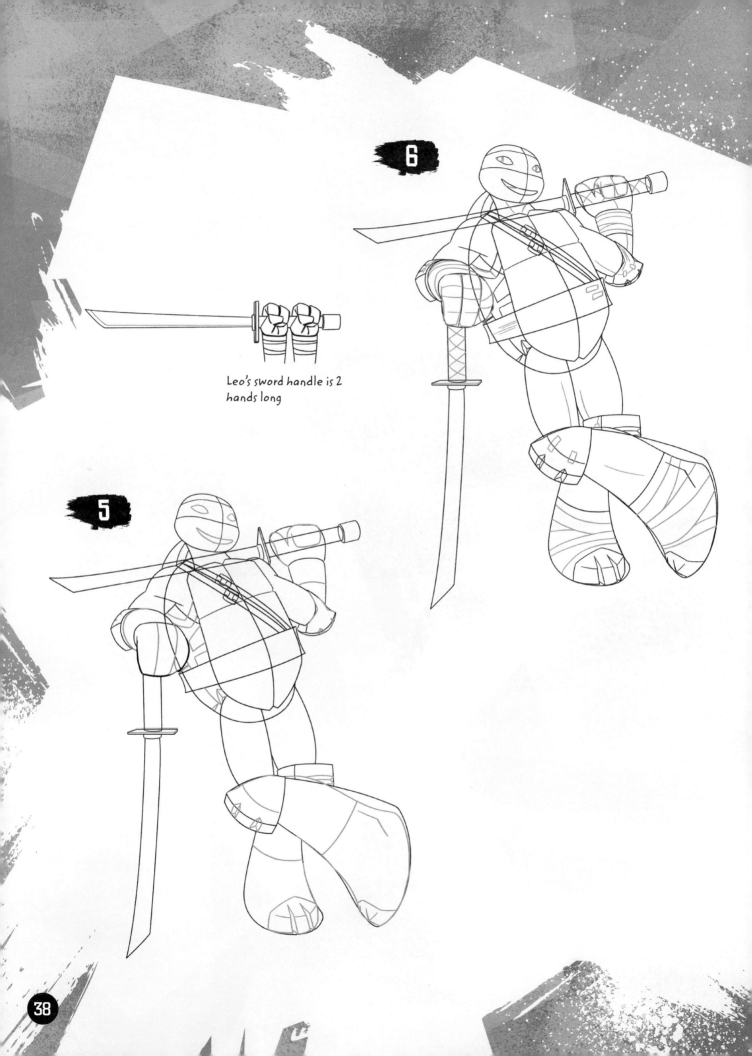

6

5

Leo's sword handle is 2
hands long

Leo's basic shapes are squares and rectangles

7

RAPHAEL

The hotheaded warrior of the group, Raph knows his skills with the sai are unmatched by anyone. So why can't his brothers acknowledge that and recognize him as the best? The only way to make them understand is to be the greatest.

1

2

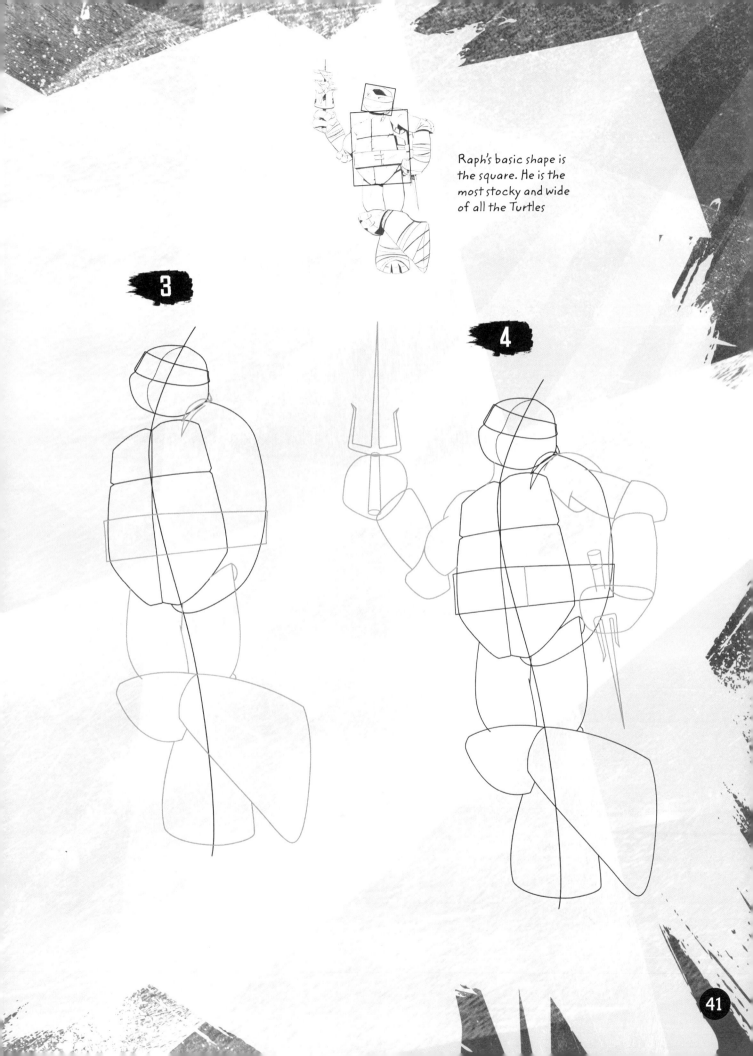

Raph's basic shape is
the square. He is the
most stocky and wide
of all the Turtles

3

4

5

6

Raph has lots of
battle damage on his
shell and clothing

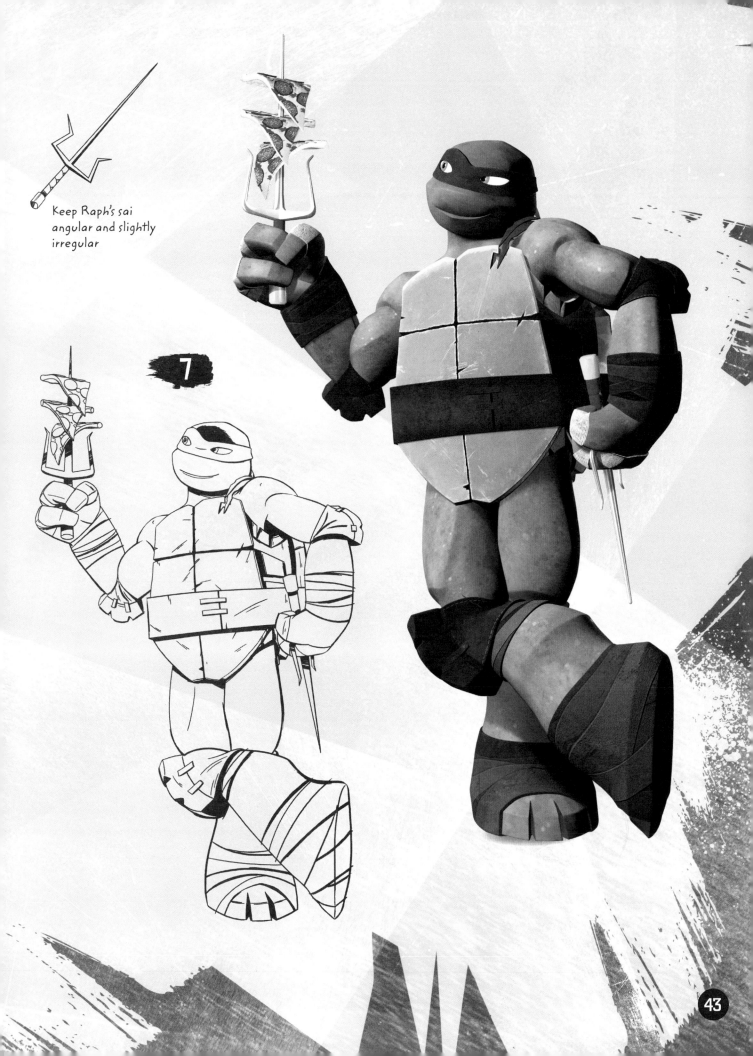

Keep Raph's sai angular and slightly irregular

7

MICHELANGELO

Mikey is definitely the most fun of all the brothers. He loves video games, skateboarding, pranking the other guys, and duh, pizza!

1

2

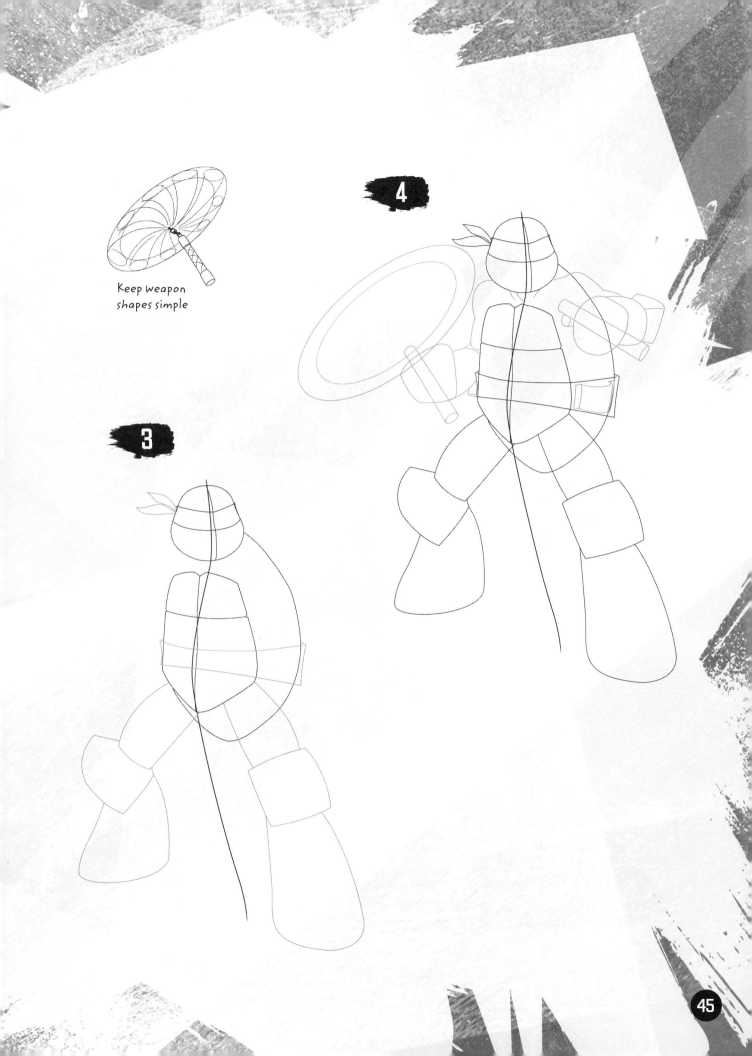

Keep weapon
shapes simple

4

3

5

6

Mike is the roundest
of the turtles

7

DONATELLO

Donnie is the brains of this outfit. He's as good a fighter as his brothers, but his real strength is his mind. His "do-it-yourself" attitude leads to exploration of the sewers, reconstructing garbage into computers, and making a TV with three whole channels. The only thing he can't figure out is how to get the Turtles' human friend, April, to notice him.

1

2

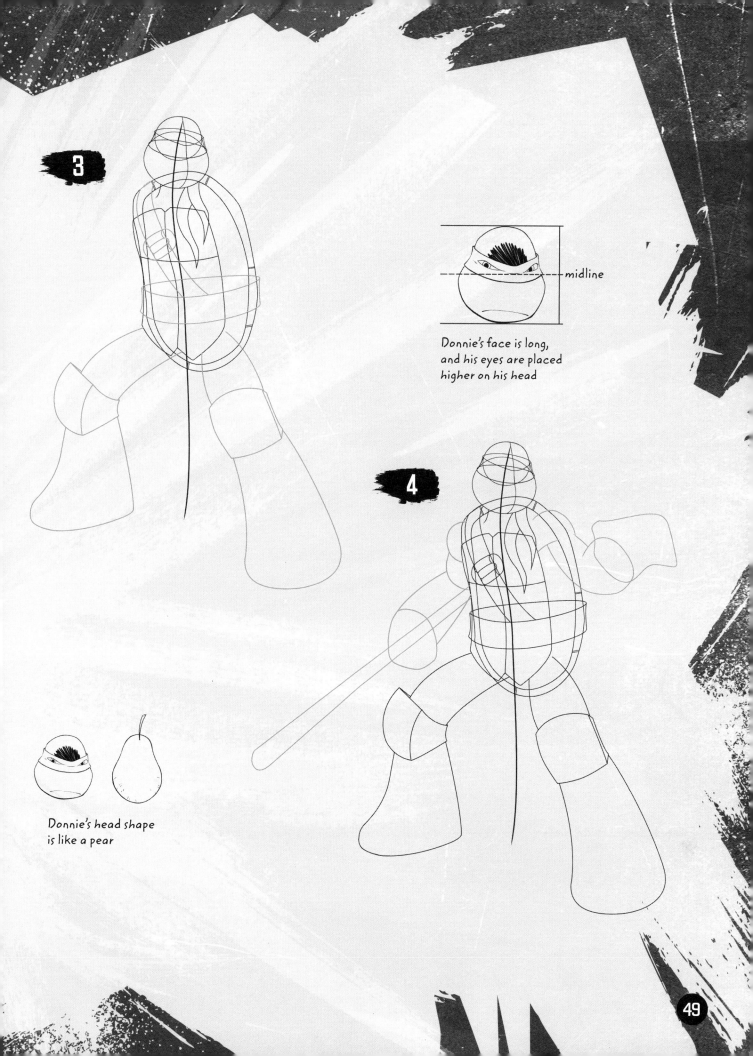

3

midline

Donnie's face is long,
and his eyes are placed
higher on his head

4

Donnie's head shape
is like a pear

5

6

AANG

Aang is an adventurous, free-spirited 12-year-old and the only known survivor of the Air Nomads. As the last Airbender, Aang is destined to become the Avatar. His connection to animals and nature allows him to "listen" to the spirits around him as they guide him on his quest to bring good to the world.

STEP 1

Start with a basic circle for Aang's head. Then add guidelines for his facial features. Next draw a curved line for his spine.

STEP 2

Extend Aang's face, and add his ear and neck; then sketch the basic shape of the torso. Make sure his right shoulder is slightly higher than his left.

Yes! Eyes are wide open—not droopy

STEP 3

Add Aang's arms, with the right arm raised so the hand and ear are the same level. Then add his legs and feet. Just follow the blue lines!

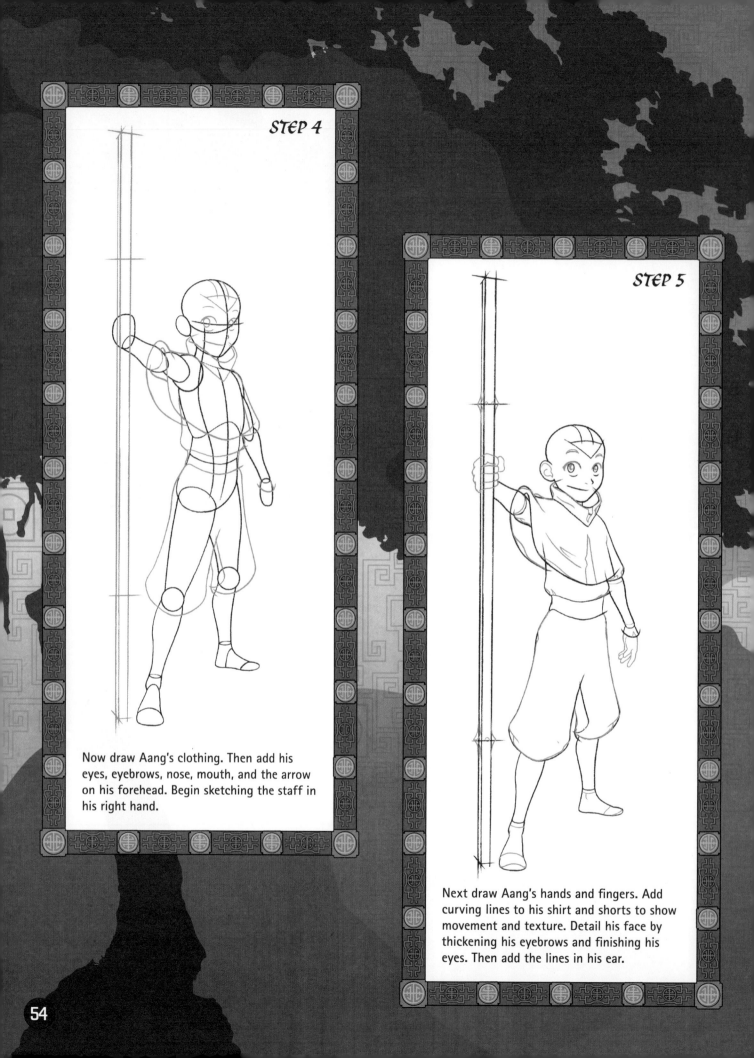

STEP 4

Now draw Aang's clothing. Then add his eyes, eyebrows, nose, mouth, and the arrow on his forehead. Begin sketching the staff in his right hand.

STEP 5

Next draw Aang's hands and fingers. Add curving lines to his shirt and shorts to show movement and texture. Detail his face by thickening his eyebrows and finishing his eyes. Then add the lines in his ear.

STEP 6

Arrow extends all the way down the back of his head (and down his back!)

Carefully erase any stray pencil lines. Darken the outline with a fine-tip black marker or the sharp point of your pencil. Then add vibrant color to give Aang life.

KATARA

Despite losing her mother at a young age, Katara has grown up to become a caring and passionate young woman. Her kindness is apparent in all aspects of her life, especially in her desire to save her tribe by becoming a Master Waterbender. Katara always wears her mother's necklace as a reminder of her mother's goodwill and loving spirit.

Thick eyelash line

Eye shape is feminine

Braid has eight bumps

STEP 1

To draw Katara, begin with a basic circle for her head. Add facial guidelines and a curved line for her spine.

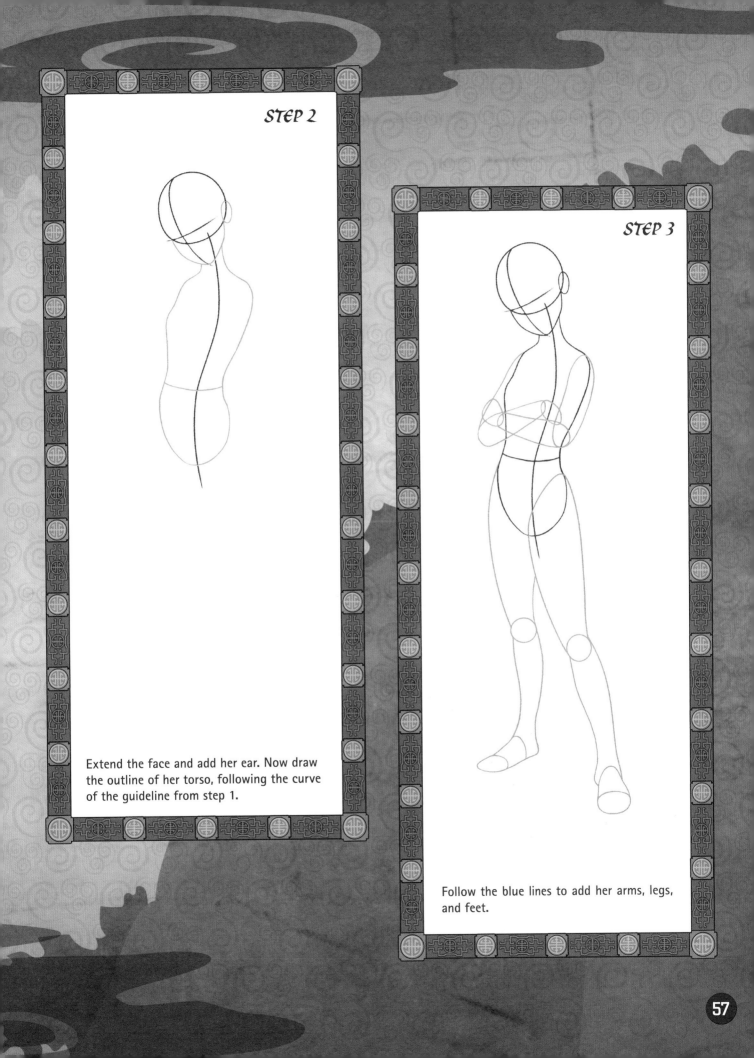

STEP 2

Extend the face and add her ear. Now draw the outline of her torso, following the curve of the guideline from step 1.

STEP 3

Follow the blue lines to add her arms, legs, and feet.

Hair pieces from front of head attach to the bun at back of head

STEP 4

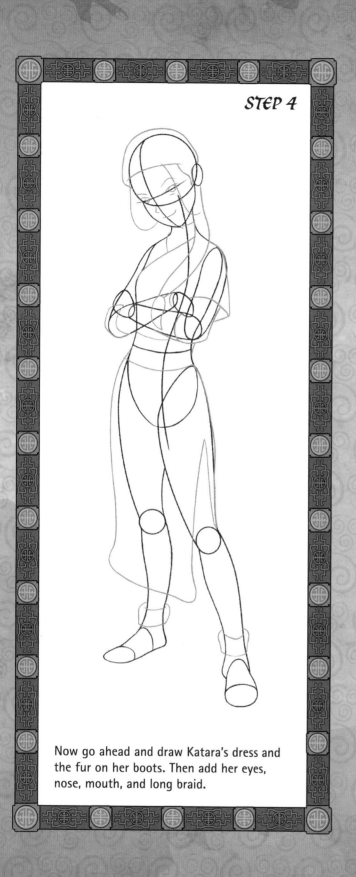

Now go ahead and draw Katara's dress and the fur on her boots. Then add her eyes, nose, mouth, and long braid.

STEP 5

Finish her dress and shoes. Add details to her hair, face, and hand. Then draw her choker.

STEP 6

Carefully erase any stray pencil lines. Then use color to dress Katara in royal blues. Her eyes match her dress!

SOKKA

Katara's brother, Sokka, is a loyal friend. Although he can be stubborn, his strength and determination are clearly visible in his actions and behavior toward others. He is practical, preferring the physical world to the spiritual, and would rather practice throwing his prized boomerang than waterbending.

Sokka wears his hair in a small ponytail

STEP 1

After drawing the circle, add the guidelines for Sokka's head and body.

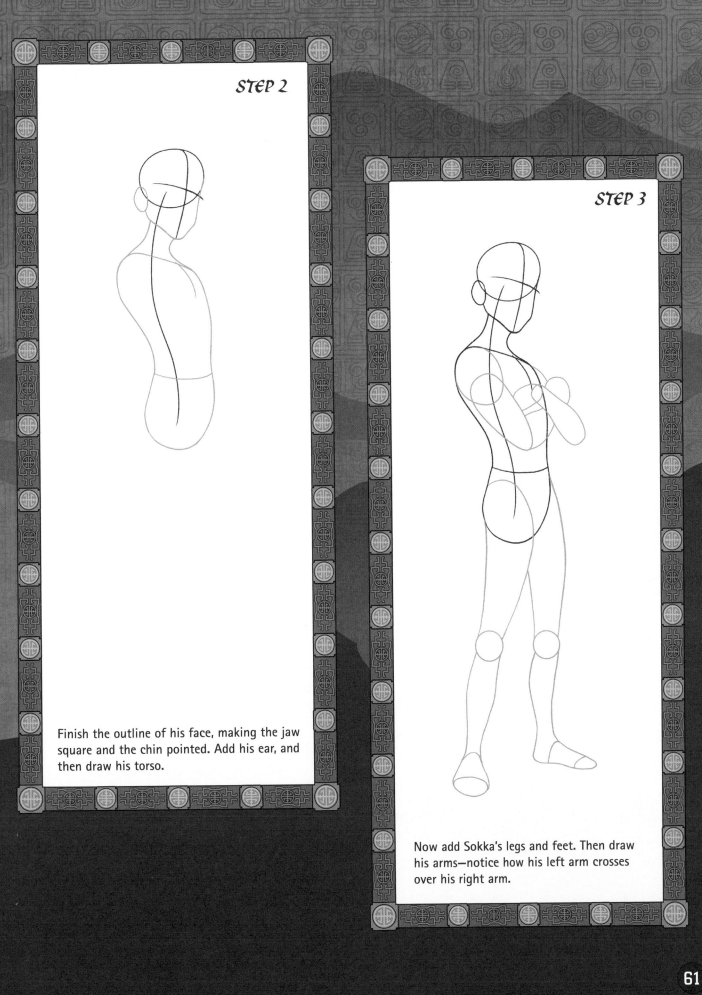

Finish the outline of his face, making the jaw square and the chin pointed. Add his ear, and then draw his torso.

STEP 3

Now add Sokka's legs and feet. Then draw his arms—notice how his left arm crosses over his right arm.

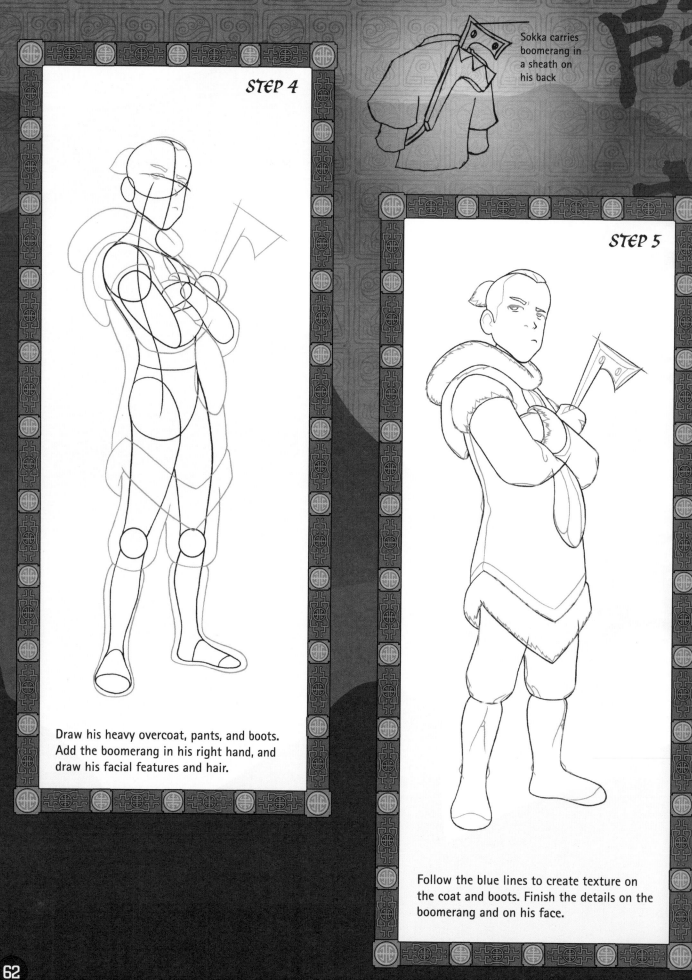

Sokka carries boomerang in a sheath on his back

Draw his heavy overcoat, pants, and boots. Add the boomerang in his right hand, and draw his facial features and hair.

Follow the blue lines to create texture on the coat and boots. Finish the details on the boomerang and on his face.

STEP 6

Carefully erase any stray pencil lines or guidelines. Then add some icy blues. Don't forget to color his boomerang!

THE END

Now that you've learned how to draw your favorite Nickelodeon characters, try experimenting on your own. Remember to use your imagination— and have fun!